J796.42
RUT

W9-CVA-044

CONTENTS

In the Beginning

O n March 25, 1878, a young woman named Maria Wiinikainen ran across frozen Lake Peuranka in Finland, covering a distance of 355 Swedish cubits (about 218 meters) in 48 seconds. That is all that is known about her. In the 120-plus years that have passed, no one has ever found an older *timed* account of a women's athletic event, so Maria is recognized by the International Amateur Athletic Federation (IAAF) as the first record holder in the history of women's track and field. We do know that her time was bettered by five seconds a few months later by a girl named Johanna, whose last name has unfortunately faded into history. Given the competitive spirit of athletes, though, it is safe to assume that Ms. Wiinikainen was none too pleased when she received the news.

Women's track and field as we know it actually dates back to the 1880s and 1890s, when women's sports clubs began to form in Great Britain and Scandinavia, and women's colleges in the United States began to hold "field days" for their students. It did not occur to anyone to keep track of times and distances back then (only the order of finish) so the records in various events are pretty sketchy.

Not until the birth of national competitions and organized track meets—in the first two decades of the 20th century—do any meaningful records actually appear. And not until the Olympics of 1928 was there track and field competition on a truly international scale. Ironically, the 1928 Summer Games, which were held in the Dutch city of Amsterdam, did more to hurt women's track than help it. In the 800 meters, several contestants collapsed and required medical attention, leading many anti-feminists to call for an end to women's events in the Olympics. Cooler heads prevailed, however, and women's events were kept in the program for the '32 games in Los Angeles. It certainly helped that in the five competitions staged in 1928, five world records were set.

Women's track and field grabbed headlines for the first time at the 1932 U.S. Championships, when a schoolgirl named Mildred "Babe" Didrikson entered as a one-woman team representing Employers Casualty Company of Texas. Didrikson finished first in five of

Babe Didrikson won the gold in the javelin during the 1932 Olympics and went on to play pro baseball, basketball, and golf.

The 1936 U.S. Olympic women's track and field team, which went on to capture two medals in Berlin. Front row, left to right: Harriett Bland, Evelyn Ferrara, Simone Schaller, Olive Hasenfus, Tidye Pickett, Betty Burch, Josephine Warren. Back row, left to right: Helen Stephens, Martha Worst, Alice Arden, Annette Rogers, D. Boeckmann (a coach and a manger), Katherine Kelly, Anne O'Brien, Gertrude Wilhelmson, Betty Robinson, Louise Stokes.

the eight events she entered and won the meet by eight points over the second-place team, which consisted of 22 athletes. In Los Angeles, she set or tied world records in all three events she entered—javelin, high jump, and 80-meter hurdles—and walked away with two gold medals and a silver. Babe might have won five medals, but at the time women were only allowed to compete in three events.

Two of the more intriguing runners of the pre-World War II era were Stella Walsh and Helen Stephens. Walsh ruled the track for the first half of the 1930s, winning a gold medal in the 100 meters at the 1932 Olympics and setting 11 world records in her career. Stephens, who emerged as a force in 1935, was a six-foot-tall sprinter who also specialized in the long jump and shot put. After she edged Walsh in the 100 meters at the 1936 Olympics, German chancellor Adolf Hitler asked to meet her, and later invited her to his place for the weekend. She declined.

Stephens did agree to a sex test after one journalist claimed she was a man, and she passed. Ironically, it was Walsh who should have been subjected to this test. In 1980, she was caught in the crossfire of a botched robbery at a Cleveland discount store. Walsh was struck by a stray bullet and killed. A routine post-mortem examination revealed she was actually a man!

Another great sprinter during this era was Betty Robinson. In her first 100-yard race, the 16-year-old high-school student tied the world record of 12 seconds. Later that year, in the 1928 Olympics, she won the gold medal in the 100 meters and silver in the 4 x 100 meters relay. Robinson spent the next three years working toward the '32 Olympics, winning several national titles and setting world records at four distances. In 1931, she was badly injured in a plane crash. After emerging from a seven-week coma, she spent two years rehabilitating her crushed limbs and then returned to the track. Robinson could no longer get down in a sprinter's crouch, but she could still run like the wind, so she concentrated on relay races. She made the U.S. Olympic squad in 1936 and anchored the relay team that upset the record-holding Germans for the gold medal.

The years following World War II saw records tumble in every event. Holland's Fanny Blankers-Koen dominating everything from the sprints to the hurdles to the long jump. In the 1950s, a pair of Australian sprint-

Wilma Rudolph scores a victory in the 100 meters during the 1960 Olympics.

ers, Marjorie Jackson and Betty Cuthbert, scored major wins in international competition. Yet the first athlete during this era to truly capture the public's imagination did not come along until the end of the decade.

Her name was Wilma Rudolph, and she had overcome childhood polio to become the fastest woman in the world. From 1956 to 1962 she was the dominant figure in American track and field, as well as the first African-American to become the unchallenged queen of her sport. After winning three gold medals at the 1960 Olympics, Rudolph was named International Athlete of the Year. In 1961 she won the Sullivan Award, as America's top amateur athlete.

Rudolph's stunning success revitalized women's track and field in the U.S. and helped programs grow in some of the poorest areas of the country. Following in her footsteps were great competitors like Wyomia Tyus and Edith McGuire, who were roommates in college. Tyus won gold in the 1964 and 1968 Olympics, and competed well into the 1970s.

Just as impressive as the American track and field athletes of the 1950s and 1960s were the ones coming out of Eastern Bloc sports programs during this time. Indeed, a new world champion seemed to emerge from behind the "Iron Curtain" almost every year. Romania's Iolanda Balas owned the high jump, winning 140 straight competitions from the mid 1950s to the mid 1960s. Soviet shot putter Galina Zybina won gold in the 1952 Olympics and was a threat to win every meet she entered right into the mid 1960s. Her countrywoman, Nina Ponomaryeva, twice won Olympic gold in the discus, while a third Soviet athlete, Tamara Press was a champion in both events. Another multitalented competitor during this time was Poland's Irena Szewinska. She won Olympic medals in five different events during the 1960s and 1970s. The star of the East German program, Ruth Fuchs, was the big name in javelin for most of the 1970s.

After the 1970s, Olympic boycotts by the U.S. (1980) and Soviet Union (1984) diminished the excitement of women's track and field somewhat. However, a number of terrific athletes emerged during this period. East Germany's Marita Koch and Marlies Gohr ruled the 100 meters until American Evelyn Ashford and Jamaica's Merlene Ottey came along to challenge them. In 1984, fans began to hear about a woman named Florence Griffith, who finished second in the Olympic 200 meters that year to veteran Valerie Brisco-Hooks. Another eye-opening performance at the '84 Summer Games was turned in by Jackie Joyner, who missed winning the gold medal in the heptathlon by the slimmest of mar-

Norway's Grete Waitz waves to the crowd after winning the silver medal in the women's marathon at the 1984 Summer Olympics.

gins. Her brother, Al, did win gold, in the triple jump. After the Olympics, Al married Florence Griffith and Jackie married her coach, Bob Kersee. The names of Jackie Joyner-Kersee and Florence Griffith-Joyner would soon dominate the headlines in women's track and field.

At the 1988 Olympics, Jackie and "Flo-Jo" were joined by rising star Gwen Torrence, and veterans Ashford and Alice Brown. These runners took home five medals—two in the relays and three individually, including a pair of gold medals for Griffith-Joyner in the 100 and 200. Joyner-Kersee also won two gold medals, setting a new world record in the heptathlon and outclassing the competition in the long jump.

Women's long-distance running also came into vogue during the 1980s, with America's Joan Benoit, Norway's Grete Waitz, and Portugal's Rosa Mota grabbing most of the headlines. At the middle distances, American Mary Decker gained as much acclaim for her failures as her triumphs. In 1982, she was the world's fastest woman at every distance from 800 to 10,000 meters—an astonishing achievement. Yet she is best remembered for her dramatic fall near the end of the 3,000 meters at the 1984 Olympics, and most admired for overcoming one injury after another in her quest for redemption. These women inspired a new generation of stars, including Algeria's Hassiba Boulmerka, who in 1992 struck a huge blow for women's rights in her country by winning an Olympic gold medal in the 1500 meters.

From the mid 1980s right through the 1990s, the belle of the ball in women's track and field was Joyner-Kersee. In 1986 she became the first American woman to hold the pentathlon record when she scored 7,148 points at the Good-will Games. At the 1987 World Championships, she became the first athlete since 1924—man or

Jackie Joyner-Kersee decided to retire after winning a gold medal in the heptathlon during the 1998 Goodwill Games,

woman—to capture gold in individual event and multi-event competition, winning the long jump and pentathlon. Over the next decade Joyner-Kersee won gold medals in three different Olympics, and dominated almost every pentathlon or heptathlon she entered. She closed out her remarkable career in 1998 by winning the heptathlon at the Goodwill Games in a riveting farewell performance.

As the 1990s draw to a close, Joyner-Kersee stands as the greatest athlete in the history of women's track and field. The beauty of the sport, however, is that ultimately she is just a link in the chain. Already, there are wonderful young women who are beginning to chip away at her records. This book profiles eight of the top athletes in the world today. Some are nearing the end of long and brilliant careers, while others are just starting out. Like Maria Wiinikainen and Helen Stephens and Jackie Joyner-Kersee, they are all threads in the same vivid tapestry of courage, commitment, perseverance, and achievement.

1959–1998

On a summer day in 1988, women's track was transformed in the span of 10.49 seconds. Florence Griffith Joyner—until then a good (but not great) sprinter—did to the 100 meters what an iceberg once did to the TITANIC. She sunk the old mark so stunningly and decisively that track experts were left groping for explanations and answers.

You shave hundredths of a second off a 100 meters record, they claimed, not a full quarter of a second, as "Flo-Jo' had done. It was the equivalent of a baseball pitcher walking out to the mound one day and firing the ball past hitters at 120 miles per hour. Later that year, in the Olympics, Griffith Joyner proved she was for real, winning three gold medals and establishing a new world record for the 200 meters with a time of 21.34 seconds. At the the end of the 1998 track season, neither of these records had been broken, much less seriously threatened.

Florence Griffith Joyner and her husband Al Joyner.

Florence Griffith Joyner attracted the world's attention with her incredible speed, but she held it with her unique sense of style and class. While other competitors wore shorts, she created her own unitards, with each eye-popping design outdoing the one before it. She simultaneously graced the pages of sports and fashion magazines, and not only moved comfortably between both worlds, but helped bring those worlds together. Indeed, much of what we see athletes wearing these days can be traced back to her groundbreaking outfits. Flo-Jo's self-expression was not limited to apparel, of course. Her flowing, raven-black hair, her impossibly long nails, and her always-impeccable appearance told female athletes it was all right to be different, it was all right to be yourself. And not to be afraid of being a woman.

In September of 1998, Florence Griffith Joyner died suddenly, unexpectedly, and horribly. A seizure suffered while she was sleeping left her incapacitated, and she suffocated under her own pillow. She had stopped racing in the mid 1990s to concentrate on her professional and personal life beyond the limits of track. Sadly, we never got to see what most certainly would have a super career outside the sport.

A lot of people who knew Flo-Jo believed no one was going to break her records—that all the runners chasing her were just wasting their time. How ironic that, in the end, the only thing that could run her down was that which eventually catches all of us.

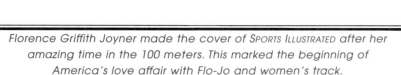

Florence Griffith Joyner made the cover of SPORTS ILLUSTRATED after her amazing time in the 100 meters. This marked the beginning of America's love affair with Flo-Jo and women's track.

"I race for my family, and for my country"

Sally Barsosio

Distance running isn't just a sport in the African nation of Kenya. It's a religion. Kip Keino, the country's most celebrated athlete, started the trend in the 1960s. The mastery continued right through the 1980s, with the legendary Henry Rono setting records at distances of 3 kilometers, 5 kilometers, and 10 kilometers. Today, no race over two miles is considered world-class without at least one Kenyan runner in the field. But until quite recently, there was one glaring problem with Kenya's long-distance tradition: It didn't include women.

Sally Barsosio is one of the young women changing that. Since arriving on the scene in 1992, she has proven that women have every right to be part of the country's running heritage. The humble, hardworking Kenyan has also become a much-needed inspiration to schoolgirls nationwide, demonstrating that with self-discipline and determination one can accomplish anything.

There was not much in Sally's early childhood to suggest she would gain such phenomenal fame. She was born in 1978, in the Elgeyo Marakwet District, which is located near the eastern border of the country. Her parents, both peasant farmers, worked endless hours each day, with little to show for their back-breaking labor. Like many who lived off the land, they struggled mightily just to buy the bare essentials for Sally and her four brothers and sisters. It was this situation that provided the impetus for Sally's sports career.

Behind Sally's schoolgirl shyness lurks the heart of a seasoned competitor.

Sally opens a slim lead on fellow Kenyan Tegla Loroupe at the 1998 Goodwill Games. Laroupe, a two-time winner of the New York City Marathon, edged Sally by 180 meters in this race.

In Kenya, where running passes for a "national pastime," there are few formal track meets for young athletes. There are many competitions held within cities and districts, however, most of which offer small cash prizes to the winners. Around the age of 10, Sally, who could run long after her friends pooped out, decided to enter some of the races. The longer the race, the better she did, and soon she was beating older girls—and making more money than her parents. Everything Sally earned went toward supporting the family. Family is everything in Kenya, and the Barsosio clan was no exception. In fact, to this day, a large percentage of her earnings goes to pay tuitions for her younger siblings, who are attending top Kenyan schools.

Sally moved into the mainstream in 1992, after she turned 14. Exposed to formal coaching for the first time, she made dramatic improvements in her technique and increased her already amazing endurance.

A year later, Sally was the surprise winner of the World Junior Cross-country Championship. Next, she stunned everyone in track—and became a national heroine—when she won a bronze medal in the 10,000 meters at the World Championships. No 15-year-old had ever done so well at this meet; the International Amateur Athletic Federation (IAAF) immediately inducted Sally into its Hall of Fame.

In 1995, Sally entered the 10,000 meters at the All-Africa Games and left the field far behind to win her first gold medal.

You might think that, with the 1996 Olympics approaching, the people running Kenya's heralded track program would have done everything they could to get Sally ready for Atlanta. But that was not the case. By and large, she did not have access to the best coaches. In the country's male-dominated culture, many feel that women should fill subservient roles. In sports, these individuals point to the fact that, historically, Kenya's female athletes have fallen embarrassingly short of their male counterparts. They conveniently ignored the fact that Kenyan women never had proper training or top coaches. And they dismissed Sally's gold medal—the first ever for a Kenyan woman—as a fluke.

"This is what has killed the morale of most female athletes in the country," says Byron Kipchumba, a family friend who has served as a sort of mentor to Sally since she was a child. "Because of their presumed weaknesses, they are discriminated against and looked down upon. What our girl has achieved was long overdue—as a result of bias during selection, training, and sponsorship of the country's flag bearers."

Sally chose to devote more time to her schoolwork in 1996, and thus ran an abbreviated schedule. Still, she made the Olympic team and had every intention of coming home with a medal. As it turned out, Sally fell short of

Getting Personal

Sally is the third of five children. Her younger sister, Florence, is also a distance runner. They finished first and second at the '98 National Championships in Kenya...Her uncle is Paul Koech, one of the top distance runners in Kenya...Sally attended Kenya's Singsore Girls' Secondary School. The school's headmistress, Josephine Anyango, says Sally "has shown us that women can also excel in fields previously thought to be the preserve of men"...Sally is a strong student who is devoted to her academic pursuits. She keeps up with her schoolwork by reading aboard planes en route to meets around the world..."This is an extraordinary girl," says Byron Kipchumba. "She operates on a strict routine which sees her integrating smoothly her academic and sporting programs"...Sally's biggest international win during 1998 came at a star-studded race in Chiba, Japan.

Career *Highlights*

Year	Achievement
1993	World Junior Cross-Country Champion
1993	IAAF Bronze Medalist, 10,000 Meters
1995	All-Africa Games Gold Medalist, 10,000 Meters
1997	World Champion, 10,000 Meters
1998	Goodwill Games Silver Medalist, 10,000 Meters

her goal. Her teammate, Pauline Konga, did break through, winning the silver in the 5,000 meters. That got fans excited back in Kenya, and focused serious attention for the first time on the women's running program. A year later, Sally struck a major blow for her countrywomen when she captured the first major international victory by a Kenyan woman.

It came in the 10,000 meters at the 1997 World Championships in Greece. Entering the race, Sally knew she would have to contend with the 1996 Olympic champion, Fernanda Ribeiro of Portugal. At this level, races are as much about strategy as speed; Ribeiro was both a shrewd competitor and a fast finisher. Sally decided to force her out of her comfort zone and make her play "catch-up." Sally pushed the pace early in the race, and Ribeiro stayed right with her. With about a mile left, Sally felt she had a little more left than her rival. She made her move, increasing her stride and forcing Ribeiro to expend whatever energy she had left. "From the beginning of the race I planned to go away," she remembers. "Ribeiro has a strong kick and I didn't want to wait for it."

The plan worked to perfection, and Sally was an easy winner. After three decades of sending its best female athletes to compete in nearly a dozen different sports, Kenya finally had its first bona fide women's world champion.

When Sally returned to Kenya, she was amazed at the reception. Her name and photo were in the newspapers constantly, and she was being compared to some pretty important people, including the great runners Keino and Rono, and even Nyiva Mwendwa, Kenya's first female government minister! Sally was now a role model. She spoke to groups of women and visited schools. It was quite a change from her days as a peasant girl.

An unintended result of Sally's newfound fame was that it had emboldened her competition at home. Before her stunning victory in Greece, Sally was viewed by her teammates as "one of the gang." Now they were vying to knock her off her perch. This was a classic "good-news/bad-news" situation. It was wonderful that Sally had given Kenya's female athletes the confidence-booster they so desperately needed, but it also meant she would have to keep getting better to solidify her claim as the best in the world at 10,000 meters.

This became abundantly clear at the 1998 Goodwill Games, when fellow Kenyan Tegla Loroupe surged ahead of Sally in the stretch to win the gold medal. Other talented Kenyan runners also are pressing her, including Jaqueline Maranga and Susan Kepchemi. Needless to say, it was all Sally could do just to win the 1998 Kenyan championship.

Also breathing down Sally's neck is Rose Cheruiyot, with whom she competed as a youngster. Their friendship has turned into a heated rivalry, and it has actually hurt Cheruiyot. On more than one occasion, she has burned herself out trying to beat Sally early in a race. Indeed, some say she is obsessed with outrunning Sally. Ironically, Sally trains with Rose's husband, Ismael. Personal rivalries do not seem to weigh heavily on Sally's mind. She trains to become the most intelligent runner she can be. If one of the other Kenyan women beats her, then she tries to learn from the loss. When she wins, she thinks about all the good the money and fame will do. Sally is more interested in helping her family overcome poverty and helping her country shed old attitudes.

Sally (left) was already a world-class long-distance runner by the age of 17.

ON HER MIND

"I don't feel there's any hu[rdle]
too high or any obstacle in
life I can't get over."

Gail Devers

There have been many great sprinters in the history of women's track, and quite a few great hurdlers. No one, however, has ever combined these two talents as magnificently as has Gail Devers. The gold medalist in the 100 meters at both the 1992 and 1996 Olympics, Gail also is widely regarded as the best hurdler on the planet—no small accomplishment, given that at 5' 4" she is far from the long-legged ideal for this event. Her trophy case is brimming with medals and awards, and her assault on the record books is well documented. Yet for an athlete used to moving in a straight line to achieve her goals, Gail's path to glory has been full of agonizing twists and turns. Indeed, there was a time in Gail's life when she could not have covered 100 meters without being picked up and carried.

Gail was born in 1966 and grew up outside San Diego, California. As a little girl, she loved two things: sports and teaching. When she was outdoors, she played whatever her older brother did, and developed great speed racing against his friends. Gail's indoor activities included after-school "classes" for her friends. Her mom was a teacher's aide, and Gail would borrow her materials. This was more than play—one of Gail's young "pupils" actually increased her reading level by two grades!

Gail continued to excel on the track and in the classroom at Sweetwater High. She made the track team as a long-distance runner, but soon found sprints to her liking. By her senior year she was the top hurdler and sprinter in the state, setting a national prep record in the 100-yard dash. After accepting a scholarship to UCLA, Gail began working

Gail is dynamite at any distance. Here she acknowledges the cheers after winning the 60 meters at the 1997 World Indoor Track and Field Championships.

The US Women's 4 x 100-meter relay team (from left, Marion Jones, Gail Devers, Chryste Gaines and Inger Miller) celebrates their victory at the 1997 World Track and Field Championships.

with famed coach Bob Kersee, who still works with her to this day.

Under Kersee's tutelage, Gail became an All-American. At one meet she finished first in five events: the 100- and 200-meter sprints, 100 meter hurdles, long jump, and 4 x 400 relay.

Gail made the 1988 U.S. Olympic team as a hurdler, and everyone agreed she would soon be among the best in the world in both the 100 meters and the hurdles—a rare feat indeed.

But Gail's bright future took a sudden, dark turn. At the '88 Olympics, she began to feel tired and sluggish and had trouble remembering things. Her times in the hurdles were horrible—the worst since her sophomore year in high school. After returning home, Gail took some time off, but her condition only worsened. She started to experience vision problems and at times she shook uncontrollably. She also lost 25 pounds. Gail's doctors were baffled for nearly two years. Finally, a correct diagnosis was made; she had Graves' Disease, a serious thyroid disorder.

The preferred treatment for Graves' Disease involved the use of drugs called beta-blockers. Unfortunately, these substances were banned by the International Amateur Athletic Federation. Gail did not want to give up her athletic career, so she chose a far more radical option: radiation therapy. Some people react well to this treatment, but Gail did not. It destroyed her thyroid and caused her feet to swell so much that she had to crawl around her apartment. At one point she was told that they might have to be amputated. "I love track and field so much that I don't know what I would have done had I lost my feet," she remembers.

Gail's doctors switched their approach and her illness was eventually brought under control with Cynthroit, a drug that did not violate IAAF regulations. Still, few believed she would ever race again.

At first, Gail was not sure either—a full month passed before she could take more than a few steps without crumpling to the ground in agony. She began her comeback slowly, walking around the track in her socks at first and getting a little stronger every day. By 1991, she had regained her strength, and even won a silver medal in the 100 meter hurdles at the World Championships in Tokyo. At the 1992 Olympic Trials, Gail qualified for the U.S. team both as a sprinter and hurdler. It was a remarkable comeback.

Though considered a longshot in the 100 meters, Gail made the finals. She exploded out of the blocks and stayed dead-even with the world's best runners as they sped toward the finish line. With one last lunge Gail broke the tape ahead of four other women to take the closest race of any kind in Olympic history. Ironically, she followed this dramatic victory with an equally stunning defeat. In the 100-meter hurdles, she had a comfortable lead when her foot ticked the final hurdle and she stumbled down the stretch in a desperate attempt to maintain her balance. By the time Gail

Getting Personal

Gail's father, Larry, was a Baptist minister and her mother, Alabe, was a teacher's aide...Her older brother's name is Parenthesis....Gail was a huge fan of **I Love Lucy**, and once made her father drive her to Los Angeles to look for Lucille Ball's home...During her 2 1/2-year illness, Gail's condition got so bad that her parents moved in with her. For many months, she needed to be carried around her apartment...Gail is now one of the strongest athletes in women's sports, and can reportedly squat-lift 400 pounds...Gail and Jackie Joyner-Kersee (Bob's wife) are best friends. Jackie gave Gail a pep talk right before she won the 100 meters final at the 1992 Olympics...The tragic death of Florence Griffith Joyner left Gail badly shaken. Flo-Jo was married to Jackie's brother, Al. The four athletes were very close...Every night at 9:00, a beeper goes off reminding Gail to take her thyroid medicine...She is a key part of a movement called "Gland Central," which educates Americans on the dangers of thyroid diseases...Gail loves the idea of being a role model. "Use me as an example," she says. "If you have faith and believe in yourself, anything is possible."

Career Highlights

Year	Achievement
1987	Pan Am Games Gold Medalist, 100 Meters
1988	Track & Field All-American
1992	Olympic Gold Medalist, 100 Meter Sprint
1993	World Champion, 100 Hurdles
1993	World Champion, 100 Meters
1994	US Champion, 100 Meters
1995	World Champion, 100 Hurdles
1995	US Champion, 100 Hurdles
1996	Olympic Gold Medalist, 100 Meters
1996	Olympic Gold Medalist, 4 x 100 Meter Relay
1997	World Champion, 4 x 100 Relay

skidded across the finish line on her knees, four other runners had already swept past her.

Between the 1992 and 1996 Olympics, Gail decided to concentrate more on her technique in the hurdles. Coach Kersee believed that she had the potential to be the best hurdler in history—her raw speed as a sprinter already gave her a huge advantage. The extra work paid off, and from 1993 to 1996 she was practically unbeatable. Gail became the first two-time gold medalist in the 100 meter hurdles when she won the 1993 and 1995 World Championships. In 1996 she again qualified for the U.S. Olympic team, both as a hurdler and sprinter.

Although favored to win Olympic gold in the hurdles, Gail once again made her mark as a sprinter. In the finals of the 100 meters, she held off teammate Gwen Torrence and Jamaica's Merlene Ottey to take the gold. Just as in 1992, the finish was so close that it took several minutes for an official winner to be declared. Gail's second gold medal in Atlanta came as a member of the U.S. 4 x 100 team, which included Torrence, Chryste Gaines, and Inger Miller. Unfortunately, her luck in the hurdles did not hold. Gail's footwork and timing were a little bit off, allowing three other runners to surge ahead of her. After clearing the last hurdle, she put on a fabulous burst of speed and caught up to the pack, but it was too late. Only 7/100ths of a second separated Gail from the winner, Lyudmila Engqvist, but she failed to win a medal, finishing fourth.

As the 1997 track season got under way, Gail could not seem to shake a series of nagging injuries. Hoping to give her legs a rest, she decided to put hurdling on the shelf and concentrate on the less taxing sprints. It was a good year but not a great one. Among her more notable 1997 victories was a gold medal at the World Championships as a member of the 4 x 100 relay team, which set an American record in the event. Gail won the 100 meters at the World University Games and World Indoor Championships, and beat Gwen Torrence in a thrilling 60 meters.

Though Gail entered the 1998 season with high hopes, she never quite got it going. The right calf injury that had bothered her in 1997 was not completely healed. Still, she returned to hurdling after a 20-month hiatus, giving track fans something to look forward to in 1999 and beyond. "I always loved the sprints because of the pure speed," she says of her decision. "But I also love challenges, and I am considered a hurdler. That's what I'm supposed to be by nature."

It is hard to believe, but as Gail moves into her mid-30s, she does not seem to be any slower than she was a decade ago. She can't explain it, nor can Coach Kersee. Yes, the injuries are piling up. And the schedule takes a little more out of her. But you sometimes get the feeling Gail could go on running—and winning—forever. That will not happen, of course. Sooner or later she will hang up her spikes. Until then, fans should savor every moment Gail spends on the track.

Gail (right) beats Jamaica's Merlene Ottey by the slimmest of margins to win gold in the 100 meters at the 1996 Olympics.

ON HER MIND

"I've never felt fearful...I just want to get out there and do my best."

Stacy Dragila

I n the spring of 1993, Idaho State University track coach Dave Nielsen decided to introduce the pole vault to the women's team. This event had almost no history in women's competition, so Nielsen really had no idea what kind of athlete he should be looking for. He decided that the ideal pole vaulter should have a long, well-muscled frame, good hand-eye coordination, upper-body strength, and a willingness to try something new. Stacy Dragila seemed to fit Nielsen's mold perfectly. So what happened the first time Stacy tried?

"I was in mortal terror!" she laughs. "I was afraid to let go of the pole. I was upside down. I didn't know where I was in the air."

Coach Nielsen had faith in Stacy, however. Certainly, she fit his profile. Born in Auburn, California, in 1971, Stacy first gravitated toward gymnastics. She showed promise in the sport, with great body control and flexibility, but eventually she had to quit after being diagnosed with asthma. Undaunted, she turned her attention to, of all things, *rodeo*. "Yeah," she recalls, "I was a rodeo girl on weekends—roping *goats*. It was always staked to the ground. I'd jump off my horse and run over and grab it and throw it to the ground and wrap it up. I'd feel real manly."

Actually, rodeo demanded excellent balance and hand-eye-coordination. It also proved that Stacy was willing to try something other than mainstream sports.

Stacy waves to her fans.

Stacy takes a break at the 1997 USA Track and Field championships.

By the time Stacy entered Placer High School, she was dabbling in several sports, including volleyball and track. She soon developed a special liking for track, although she wasn't quite sure where to focus her efforts. "I tried everything," Stacy recalls. "I liked the relays, I tried the hurdles, and I played around with the long jump a little bit."

After her graduation, Stacy attended Yuba Community College, where she continued to compete in track and field. The school's coach, John Orognen, noticed her all-around ability and suggested she try the heptathlon, a demanding competition that includes the hurdles, shot put, high jump, 200-meter dash, long jump, javelin, and 800-meter run. Stacy took to the heptathlon in a big way, and caught the eye of several major universities. In 1997, she was offered a scholarship to Idaho State, and she accepted.

The pole vault experiment came early the following year. That first jump, which so terrified Stacy, was all of six feet. "When I was first introduced to it—me and four other athletes—we were scared," she remembers. "It was hard to get the technique down. The others got discouraged. My coach told me to stick with it."

Stacy turned out to be a natural. Within a year she was clearing 10 feet, and by the time she graduated in 1995, she was consistently up around 12 feet. She continued to compete in the heptathlon, too, and in her senior year finished second in the Big Sky Conference.

Getting Personal

Stacy attributes her willingness to try different sports to early battles with her older brother...She has dreamed of being an Olympian since she was a kid, but originally she thought she'd go as a gymnast...Stacy believes that gymnastics training is a big advantage in her sport. "I don't know where it comes from, but a lot of women vaulters are ex-gymnasts, and they are bringing a whole new set of dynamics to it"...Unlike some in her sport, Stacy must practice vaulting constantly. If she takes more than a couple of days off, she loses the feel...Her coach, Dave Nielsen, was a top vaulter in the 1970s. He once cleared 17 feet 6 inches...During one amazing stretch in 1997, Stacy set five U.S. records in five weeks...Stacy earns a living competing on the European track circuit. Her biggest pay day has been $25,000...Her husband, Brent Mikaelson, is training to become a member of the California Highway Patrol...Stacy won six events in 1998, breaking her own American record in June.

After graduating, Stacy began working on her advanced degree in Physical Education Administration. She also threw herself into the pole vault with renewed passion, and her hard work paid off. On January 13, 1996—less than three years after her first leap—Stacy set the American indoor record for women at 12 feet, $11^3/_4$ inches. She passed the 13-foot mark the following week, and by April owned both the U.S. indoor and outdoor marks.

In pole vaulting terms, Stacy had it all. Her speed enabled her to come at the bar with tremendous momentum. Her power and coordination helped her explode as she planted the pole. And her ability to maneuver her body in midair gave her the extra inch or two she needed to beat the best in the country.

In January of 1997, Stacy cleared 14 feet. Several months later, during a meet in Paris, France, she soared to 14 feet, $5^3/_4$ inches, the best indoor leap in the history of her sport. That record did not stand long, however, for there were a couple of other top vaulters on the international scene. By the end of 1997, Stacy and Daniela Bartova of the Czech Republic jointly held the indoor mark at slightly more than 14 feet, 8 inches. The biggest challenge, however, came from Australian star Emma George. In 1998, George became the first woman to clear 15 feet.

Career *Highlights*

Year	Achievement
1996	Set First U.S. Indoor Record
1996	Set First U.S. Outdoor Record
1997	Set First World Indoor Record

The competition doesn't bother Stacy. On the contrary, she thrives on the pressure and excitement. As far as she is concerned, the more the merrier—her sport is a relatively new one, and needs the exposure. "It's been amazing how well so many Europeans are vaulting," says Stacy. "It isn't just Emma and me who jump high—there are six or eight others duking it out. It's really competitive and that's great for the sport."

Women's pole vault is on the schedule for the first time at the 1999 indoor world championships, and at the outdoor championships the following year. The hope is that it will one day be a major Olympic sport with an enthusiastic worldwide following. If the crowd reaction at the 1998 Millrose Games in New York is any measure, the future of pole vaulting should be very bright. The fans—who are among the most knowledgeable in the country—were absolutely spellbound during the pole vault competition, cheering wildly for each competitor as the bar rose higher and higher. It was one of those meets people will look back on a few years from now as a watershed event.

Stacy will no doubt be an important part of that future. She is willing to work hard and make sacrifices for her sport. In fact, she recently put her graduate studies on hold in order to devote herself fully to her electrifying duel with Emma George. Stacy recognizes you have to accept some trade-offs if you want to be a pioneer. "Sometimes I get discouraged," she admits. "I feel I'm putting a lot of other stuff on hold. But I know it's going to take some time for women vaulters to get recognized."

Stacy takes off at the 1997 U.S. Track & Field Championships.

ON HER MIND

"I just wanted to show people that I am proud of who I am and where I came from."

Cathy Freeman

A t the close of the 18th century, Australia saw its first wave of white settlers. The native Australians watched the European newcomers with interest and trepidation, much as the native Americans had more than 100 years earlier. Sadly, they suffered a similar fate. The "Aborigines," as British settlers called them, were systematically swept from their lands, and for most of the next two centuries they were abused, mistreated, and left to scratch out a meager existence in Australia's harsh "outback" region. It was not until the 1960s that the Aborigines were given full citizenship and the right to participate in the country's government; only now are they emerging from the shadow of discrimination and economic hardship.

One of the people who is helping to make this transformation possible is Cathy Freeman. Cathy is an Aborigine, and because she ranks among the fastest women in the world, she has become an important symbol of achievement. Besides blinding speed, Cathy possesses a keen understanding of who she is, where she comes from, and what it means to be an Aborigine succeeding on the world stage. While she can be an instrument of healing and reconciliation, she knows she also must be an advocate for her people. "Compared to minority groups in other countries, we haven't progressed far," says Cathy. "And this was *our* home *first*. People are now still finding their families because they were taken away from each other. That's how far behind we are!"

Cathy became the first Aborigine to win a major track title when she triumphed in the 400 meters at the 1997 World Championships.

Cathy's smooth strides and calm demeanor make winning look easy sometimes.

Born in 1973, Cathy grew up in Mackay, a small town on Australia's eastern seaboard. Like most Aborigine families, the Freemans struggled to make ends meet. Cathy distinguished herself in school as an excellent athlete, and by the age of 14 it was clear that she had the makings of a world-class sprinter. She exploded out of the blocks and generated tremendous power with her still-growing legs—all despite a lack of formal training.

That situation changed when she made Australia's 4 x 100 relay team for the 1990 Commonwealth Games, and led the squad to a gold medal with an excellent performance. Cathy blossomed into a bona fide world-class sprinter. She would soon specialize in the 400 meters, a race that combines speed, strategy, and endurance—all in the span of 50 seconds.

Cathy was named Young Australian of the Year. Aborigines, searching for strong voices in their fight for equality, found in this 16-year-old champion a powerful new symbol for their cause. She was hesitant to speak out about racial injustice at first, but soon became comfortable discussing the plight of her people.

Cathy was not the first famous Aborigine athlete, but she was the first to take such an aggressive stance. Two decades earlier, Evonne Goolagong achieved worldwide fame as a Grand Slam tennis champion. However, she chose not to focus attention on her Aboriginal roots. Cathy was a different story. Off the track, she continued to be a vocal advocate for Australia's Aborigines. Soon, everything she did and everything she said—whether meant as a political statement or not—was put into this context. To some Australians, that made her a threat.

At the 1994 Commonwealth Games, Cathy again stole the show, blowing past her fellow runners and setting a new record. To celebrate her gold-medal performance, she draped herself in the red-white-and-blue Australian and black-red-and-yellow Aboriginal flags. Cathy meant only to show her national pride. But it did not play that way back home. A firestorm of controversy ensued, as her celebration was construed by many as an act of protest and defiance. Television and radio airwaves were abuzz with debate, and many condemned Cathy's actions. "As an indigenous individual, there is no reason you can't be like everyone else and go out and achieve your goals and dreams," she explains. "That's all I wanted to represent."

As the controversy unfolded, it became increasingly clear that the vast majority of Australians—both white and Aborigine—supported Cathy, regardless of why she did what she did. Paul Keating, the Prime Minister, came to her defense. And Australian school children voted her their

Getting Personal

Cathy loves to visit schools around Australia. She had few role models in the Aboriginal community growing up, and hopes to change that situation. "Hopefully, it helps them get out the door and say, 'I'm going for that—I want to do that, be a doctor or lawyer or sprinter or whatever.' It makes them feel they've got a chance. There aren't enough people who think like that in the Aboriginal community"...In 1990, Cathy became the first Aborigine to win a gold medal at the Commonwealth Games. Six years later she became the first to represent Australia in the Olympics...After finishing second at the 1996 Olympics, Cathy gained 11 pounds and lost confidence in herself. She worked with a sports psychologist to restore her self-esteem and went on a remarkable 20-race winning streak...In 1997, she became the first Australian woman to win a world track title...Cathy is the only person ever to win the Young Australian of the Year and Australian of the Year awards.

Career Highlights

Year	Achievement
1990	Commonwealth Games Gold Medalist, 4 x 100 Relay
1990	Young Australian of the Year
1994	Commonwealth Games Gold Medalist, 200 Meters & 400 Meters
1996	Breaks 50-Second Barrier for First Time, 400 Meters
1996	Olympic Silver Medalist, 400 Meters
1996	Grand Prix Female Athlete of the Year
1997	IAAF Champion, 400 Meters
1998	Wins 20th Consecutive Race, 400 Meters
1998	Australian of the Year

favorite athlete. Cathy had learned an important lesson. She realized that, as a national symbol, she now had to think her actions through. As she moved on to the world stage, this new maturity would serve her well.

At the 1996 Olympics in Atlanta, Georgia, Cathy went up against the top runners in the world. Although she was given little more than an outside shot at a medal, when the starter's gun sounded she stayed with favorite Marie-Jose Perec stride for stride. The French superstar managed to edge Cathy at the tape, but a silver medal was better than anyone could have imagined. This time Cathy draped herself only in the Australian flag—a small gesture that paid huge dividends when she returned Down Under. Hailed as her country's brightest and most beloved sports star, she found that her voice was now reaching people who never would have listened before.

At the 1997 IAAF World Championships in Athens, Greece, Cathy made history. In the 400 final, after getting out of the blocks a little slowly, she caught up to leaders Sandie Richards and Jearl Miles and crossed the finish line first by a mere .02 seconds. Never before had an Aborigine won a major international track title. As she had done three years earlier at the Commonwealth Games, Cathy jogged a jubilant victory lap. And again, she clutched both the Australian and Aboriginal flags as she circled the stadium. This time, however, no one objected. On the medal stand, she broke into tears while the Australian anthem was played.

Cathy was later honored as Australian of the Year. As one Australian columnist later observed, in a little less than 50 seconds, she had done more for her people than had been accomplished in the previous 200 years.

Thanks in significant part to Cathy's work—both on and off the track—the idea of "Reconciliation" is a popular one in Australia today. A lot of issues that had been kept in the shadows of history are now out in the open. On both sides, prominent Australians are working to find ways to live together in harmony, and to begin healing the wounds of the past. Does Cathy see her role in this process growing? Does she plan to become more vocal, especially with the 2000 Olympics to be held in Sydney, Australia?

"I don't want to be a politician or anything like that," she says. "Kids are what's most important to me. I'm so glad of what I am, Australian and Aboriginal. They're two and the same."

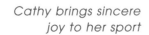

Cathy brings sincere joy to her sport

ON HER MIND

"I have to keep pushing the record up and improving."

Emma George

W hat makes a great pole vaulter? A few years ago, when women's vaulting was just getting off the ground, no one knew for sure. Some believed that small, hard-muscled athletes would fare better than longer, leaner competitors. Others thought that size was not as important as flexibility and body control. Many coaches believed that the answer lay somewhere between the two extremes, and began recruiting young women with gymnastics training who had grown too big for the sport. No one, however, was looking for former trapeze artists.

That probably is why no one ever thought to ask Emma George to give vaulting a try. In fact, it was Emma who first approached Deakin University coach Mark Stewart. She was double-majoring in Arts and Commerce at the Melbourne, Australia, college when she spotted some women attempting to clear the bar. Emma heard that Coach Stewart was looking for ex-gymnasts, and she asked him if being a former circus acrobat qualified. The rest, as they say, is history.

Stewart was intrigued by Emma's story. When she was eight years old, her parents put her in the Albury-Wodonga Flying Fruit Flies, a very popular traveling show that featured young athletes and acrobats. Emma performed with the Fruit Flies for three years, and was trained by the troupe's Chinese tumbling and gymnastics coaches. Her most spectacular stunt was doing a handstand on six stacked chairs. Later on, in high school, Emma

Emma celebrates after breaking the women's world indoor pole vault record by nearly three inches in March of 1998.

Concentration is crucial in pole vault.
Emma began to develop hers as a child acrobat.

ran sprints and competed in the long jump. So it was only natural that, at the age of 19, the opportunity to try an exotic new sport caught her imagination. "I thought it would be fun to give it a go," she recalls.

Within a matter of months, Coach Stewart had Emma clearing the bar at 12 feet. Within a year, she was approaching world-class standards. It helped that Emma had an excellent understanding of the sport. She recognized immediately that women actually had a couple of advantages over men, and that the focus of her technique and training should be different from what male vaulters were being taught. Women have a lower center of gravity, which enables them to swing more freely at the top of the vault. What do they lack compared to men?

"Great upper body strength," Emma says.

To close this gap, Emma embarked upon a regimen designed to increase the strength in her arms, chest and shoulders. She did a lot of circuit training, with a heavy emphasis on chin-ups. Meanwhile, she began drawing on her experience as a high-flying circus performer and began tinkering with new ways of clearing the bar. Emma began winning almost every competition she entered, and set her first world record in November of 1995—less than two years after her first jump.

Getting Personal

Emma has dreamed of representing her country since childhood. "I've wanted to have an Australian vest since I was about five years old"...The circus troupe she joined as a child did not take her away from academics. The Flying Fruit Flies scheduled practices and tours so as not to interfere with school...Although the women's vault mark is still five feet lower than the men's, Emma believes that women might one day jump higher...Emma's greatest disappointment came in 1997, during her first tour of Europe. She sprained an ankle and had to return to Australia...When she is not flying through the air, Emma can be found knee-deep in a river. She loves to go fishing.

The 1996 and 1997 seasons saw the women's mark climb higher and higher, from 14 feet to nearly 15. Emma was among a group of top vaulters who seemed to break the world record almost every week. Meanwhile, she had become the figurehead of her sport in Australia. It was quite an honor to have other vaulters learning from her, but Emma felt that *she* needed to be a student in order to learn even more. She decided to take a break from school and join an elite group of pole vaulters coached by Alex Parnov. She would train and learn with Dmitri Markov and Viktor Chistyakov, two of the best vaulters in the world. "The benefit of training with Alex is that he has two excellent male athletes," she explains. "It's a good opportunity to learn new drills and ideas, and improve my technique."

The strategy paid off in 1998, when Emma became the first woman to clear 15 feet. She made the most of Australia's summer track season (which takes place in February and March), establishing a new outdoor

Career *Highlights*

Year	Achievement
1995	Sets First World Outdoor Record
1998	First Woman To Clear 15 Feet

record five times in five weeks. Then Emma hit the international circuit, where she went head-to-head with the likes of Stacy Dragila, Daniela Bartova, Anzhela Balakhonova, and Yelena Belyakova.

The competition only made her better. Of the 20 best jumps in 1998, 11 belonged to Emma. She won more than a dozen major competitions to establish herself as the woman to beat in her sport.

Although Emma enjoys competing at both indoor and outdoor events, the most important record to her is the outdoor mark. "It's more important for me to hold the outdoor record because the Commonwealth Games, the Olympics, and World Championships are all outdoors."

Whether Emma can keep dominating remains to be seen. The indoor and outdoor records seem to tumble every month—sometimes several times a month. Even though it is Emma who keeps edging the bar up, there are plenty of talented vaulters right behind her. Actually, the thing she likes most about her sport is how the competitors relate to one another, and especially how they approach their craft. Unlike male vaulters, who rely heavily on raw power and adrenaline, the women are true students of their sport. And each brings something a little different to the competition—including a great attitude. Indeed, Emma and the others enjoy a camaraderie that is rare in track and field. The vaulters actually look forward to seeing one another at the big events and sharing their insights and discoveries. "The pole vault is special because competitors need to help each other at times," she explains. "Also, since you're out there for two to three hours at a time, why *not* be friendly?"

As Emma prepares for the 2000 Olympics in her home country, she knows her friends will be gunning for her. Additionally, she realizes that the eyes and expectations of millions of Aussies will be fixed on her. Many believe she is Australia's best hope for a gold medal. Does she feel the pressure?

"To be honest, yes," she admits. "But I'm trying not to think about it. The main thing is for me to relax, focus on doing the best I can and enjoy the experience. To be in an Olympics is something special, but to go into a stadium in your own country with over a hundred thousand people screaming for you? That'll be just great!"

Emma clears the bar at a Grand Prix event in Japan. She has become one of the most popular female athletes in the world.

ON HER MIND

"My whole life I've wanted to be distinguished in something, to be great."

Marion Jones

F or an entire generation of sports fans, the initials MJ meant one thing and one thing only: Michael Jordan. Will that remain true for the next generation? Not if Marion Jones has her way. Like Jordan, she has singlehandedly brought her sport into the international spotlight, and may already be the best athlete it has ever seen.

Actually, Marion and Michael have something else in common: Both were All-American guards for the University of North Carolina. After the 1997 basketball season, Marion had to make a decision: join one of the women's pro hoops leagues, or devote herself to track. She chose track, threw herself into training, and seven weeks later won the 100 meters and long jump at the U.S. Championships. After that, she went to Athens to take on the greatest athletes in the world at the World Championships. She left Greece with gold medals in the 100 meters and 4 x 100 relay.

Track insiders remembered Marion; she had once been a prodigy. The rest of the world, however, was in shock. How could someone so good come out of "nowhere?"

Of course, everyone comes from *somewhere*—in Marion's case, that was Los Angeles, California. As far as her athletic ability is concerned, that remains a mystery. No one on either side of her family has ever displayed much aptitude in sports. Her mother emigrated from the Central American nation of Belize and married Marion's dad, who was originally from Louisiana. Marion became interested in sports thanks to her older brother, Albert. "He was always involved in athletics with his friends,"

Marion takes a breather after winning the 800-meter event at the 1998 Penn Relays.

Marion believes she has yet to tap her potential in the long jump.

remembers Marion. "I got exposed to a lot of sports and loved them all."

Both children participated in many activities, but Marion had an eerie ability to master everything she tried, from T-ball to tap dancing. Albert introduced her to track, and she soon joined a track club coached by a man named Jack Dawson. He had seen her playing basketball—dribbling faster than the other girls could run!—and knew right then she would be a great one. By the age of 10, Marion was the national champion in her age group; by age 12, she was competing in international events; by 15, she was running the 100 meters in under 11.2 seconds and the 200 in under 23.8. At the age of 16, Marion actually qualified for the U.S. Olympic team as an alternate in the relay. Her mother decided she was too young to go.

In high school, Marion established a new national prep record for the 200 meters, then broke her own mark four times before she graduated. She came within an eyelash of breaking the 100 meters and long jump records, too.

Marion's accomplishments were not limited to track. She was an excellent student and one of the top basketball players in the city. This combination turned out to be the winning one for Marion, as she chose to attend the University of North Carolina on a basketball scholarship.

Marion led the Lady Tar Heels to the 1994 national championship with her passing, scoring, and tenacious defense. She also competed in track that spring, and finished second in the long jump at the NCAA Championships. In 1995, Marion concentrated mainly on basketball, but with the Olympics coming to the U.S. in August of 1996, she began to plan a return to track.

Then disaster struck. In the summer of 1995, during tryouts for the World University Games basketball team, she broke her foot. A 2-inch screw was inserted to strengthen the bone, but while Marion was training on a trampoline a few months later, the screw bent, ruining any chance she had of making the U.S. track squad in time for the Olympics.

Marion finished her basketball career at Carolina in fine form, averaging 18.1 points per game and earning All-America recognition. She graduated with a degree in Journalism and Communications. With the WNBA and ABL gearing up, Marion's next move seemed obvious—to everyone *but* Marion. "I had to decide then what to do with my life," she says, "play basketball or run track. I chose track. It was always my first love."

Marion began training, trying to recapture all that she had lost. She felt greatness was still within her, but could not coax it back out. Then,

Getting Personal

Marion's parents divorced when she was just a baby. Her mom remarried, but her stepfather died when Marion was in sixth grade...Because her mother is originally from Belize, Marion holds dual citizenship in the U.S. and Belize. She still visits that country often...Marion was so famous in high school that famed lawyer Johnnie Cochran once intervened on her behalf when he heard that a technical glitch in a drug testing procedure might keep her from competing in a meet...Marion's senior stats in basketball were 22.8 points and 14.7 rebounds per game. She played forward...Talk about dedication! Marion had to cancel her date on the night of the senior prom, because she had a game...Marion's coach, Trevor Graham, says what separates her from the rest is not her legs, but her head. She understands that a sprint is built one step at a time, and the better each step becomes, the better the result...Marion believes she can add many inches to her personal best in the long jump, because she is still learning the event. "I have no idea what a good long jump feels like," she says. "The sky's the limit for me—if I get a good jump the world record is gone."

Career Highlights

Year	Achievement
1991	National High School Player of the Year, Track & Field
1992	National High School Player of the Year, Track & Field
1993	National High School Player of the Year, Track & Field
1994	NCAA Champion, Basketball
1997	U.S. Champion, 100 Meters & Long Jump
1997	World Champion, 100 & 200 Meters
1998	U.S. Champion, 100 Meters, 200 Meters & Long Jump
1998	Goodwill Games Gold Medalist, 100 and 200 Meters
1998	World Cup Champion, 100 & 200 Meters
1998	Won 37 Consecutive Events

one day, she had a chance meeting with destiny while working out with her boyfriend, C.J. Hunter. A free-lance track coach named Trevor Graham happened to be at the same track. Though not affiliated with a school, track club, or shoe company, Graham had developed a reputation as a running "guru." He watched Marion train for a few minutes, asked her some questions, then made a couple of simple suggestions. "In five minutes," Hunter remembers, "Trevor showed her more than she'd learned in her whole life."

One very important lesson Marion learned was how to "relax" in a short race—just the opposite of what most sprinters do. "You can only run fast if you stay relaxed," she explains. "Tense up and you can't attain full range of motion. When you're really running well, your arms and face are relaxed—you feel like you're cutting through clouds."

That is certainly how Marion looked in 1997. At the World Championships that year, Jones was viewed as a raw rookie. In the 100 meters final, old hands Merlene Ottey and Zhanna Pintusevich did their best to unnerve her. But after the runners broke the tape, it was *Marion* who looked like the unflappable veteran. While awaiting the result of the photo finish, Pintusevich draped herself in the Ukrainian flag and hopped around the stadium like a schoolgirl, assuming she had won. Marion calmly, coolly waited for the announcement. She, not

Pintusevich, was the winner. Marion covered for her embarrassed rival by saying how easy it is to get carried away in the excitement of a big meet.

Marion remained calm and cool throughout 1998, when she began to realize her immense potential. At the U.S. Championships, she equaled a 50-year-old record by taking the 100 meters, 200 meters, and long jump. Her time in the 100 was a meet record, as was her winning jump. Simply competing in three events is a great achievement. Blowing everyone else away in those events is just remarkable.

Marion got stronger as the season progressed. She took the 100 and 200 at the Goodwill Games, and at the World Cup in Johannesburg, South Africa, she ran the 100 in 10.65 seconds. In all of history, only Florence Griffith Joyner had run this race faster. At that point, Marion had won 36 events in a row during 1998. She won the 200 meters to make it 37, then lost in the long jump (on a rain-slicked track) for her only defeat of the year.

So what kind of goals do you have when it seems you have already achieved everything? Marion wants to win five Olympic gold medals, and she thinks there is a chance she will do it all at once, in Sydney. She also believes she can surpass her idol, Jackie Joyner-Kersee, and leave track as its greatest athlete ever. "I definitely don't deserve that title yet," says Marion, who always seems to teeter between supreme confidence and quiet humility. "I still consider Jackie the best—and probably will until the end of my life."

Marion (right) is a picture of power and concentration when she runs the 100 meters.

ON HER MIND

"you just have to think positively and stay mentally strong."

Inger Miller

L ennox Miller was a bona fide legend in his country. He was the star of the Jamaican track team in the 1960s and 1970s, winning a silver medal in the 100 meters at the 1968 Olympics, then taking the bronze four years later in Munich by diving across the finish line. A few weeks before his dramatic finish, Lennox's daughter, Inger, was born in California.

Inger's dad had earned a degree in dentistry at the University of Southern California, and after the Olympics the Millers decided to set down roots in this part of the United States. Inger turned out to be a sports maniac, excelling in soccer, volleyball, softball, and basketball. By her 11th birthday, there seemed to be no doubt that she had a future in sports. But which one?

The answer came after she transferred to Muir High School in 1987. The track coach noticed Inger racing up and down the field during a soccer game, and asked her if she would consider trying out for his team. She made the Muir High squad easily, and by season's end had qualified for the 1988 state championships—where she finished second in the 100 meters and third in the 200. She also participated in the trials for the Jamaican Olympic squad that year, and narrowly missed making the team. By the time she finished high school, Inger was one of the hottest runners in the country.

Inger celebrates making the U.S. team at the 1996 Olympic trials.

Inger tries her hand at television commentary for FOX.

Dozens of colleges expressed interest in Inger, and she thought their scholarship offers over carefully. But in the end she chose to follow in her father's footsteps and attend USC. "I went on recruiting trips," she says. "But I was always a Trojan. It would have been very hard for me to go anywhere else."

With the symbolic torch now passed from father to daughter, the path for Inger seemed clear: break a few records at USC, capture an NCAA title or two, win an Olympic medal and then achieve fame and fortune on the international track circuit. Unfortunately, this is where the Inger Miller story took a strange and sorry turn.

Inger was plagued by injuries her freshman year, pulling a groin muscle and suffering a number of foot problems. Still, when healthy, she ran the 100 in just over 11 seconds. Her sophomore year was also marred by injuries, as a pulled hamstring kept her out of the NCAA Championships and—even worse—the 1992 Olympic trials. Inger's junior year showed a glimmer of hope, as she turned in the top times in the world during 1993 for both the 100 and 200 meters. But another injury cut her season short before the NCAA Championships. Again, she was getting better and gaining experience, but had nothing to show for it.

The final straw came during Inger's senior year, when she rebroke the foot that she had initially hurt in 1991. This time, it required surgery. "When I saw the stitching, how big the foot was, I thought, 'Oh, God, this is never going to be right again,'" Miller recalls.

After six months of rehabilitation, Inger was back on the track. But she had lost her edge, both physically and mentally. To have any chance of making the U.S. Olympic team in 1996, she would have to mount an unprecedented comeback. Knowing that she needed someone who understood both her body and mind, she turned to her father and asked him to be her coach. The two embarked on an aggressive training schedule.

The Millers formed a powerful package of talent and experience. Inger made astonishing progress, not only regaining her former abilities, but far surpassing them. She was faster, stronger, and smarter—a combination that enabled her to qualify for the Olympics in the 200 meters and 4 x 100 relay.

Inger would be the first to admit that she was lucky to make it to the Olympics—not because she didn't deserve to, but because the bad luck bug bit her yet *again*. That May, she got behind the wheel of her sport utility vehicle and pulled onto the 605 Freeway near her home. While she was traveling around 60 mph, another car suddenly veered in front of her.

Getting Personal

Inger has a younger sister named Heather, who also runs track...Inger won a total of six Pacific League track titles while at Muir High...Her late start in the sport came about because the first high school she attended, the Westridge School, did not have a track team...At USC, Inger earned a degree in Biological Science...Earlier in her career, she was often introduced at meets as "the daughter of Lennox Miller"...Inger's godfather, Don Quarrie, was also an Olympian. He won the gold medal in the 200 meters in 1976...Her father now practices in Pasadena, and is an assistant professor at the USC School of Dentistry. He once held the school record for the fastest time in the 100 meters...Inger remembers watching tapes of her dad when she was a kid. She was less impressed with how he ran than with how he looked. "We'd say, 'Oh my God, that's dad—look at his hair!'"...When Inger retires, she plans to become a veterinarian.

Career *Highlights*

Year	Achievement
1988	Pacific League High School Champion, 100 and 200 Meters
1989	Pacific League High School Champion, 100 and 200 Meters
1990	Pacific League High School Champion, 100 and 200 Meters
1996	#1 Ranked American, 200 Meters
1996	Olympic Gold Medalist, 4 x 100 Relay
1998	IAAF Grand Prix Champion, 4 x 100 Relay

When Inger attempted to swerve out of harm's way, she lost control. Her SUV began to tumble, over and over and over. "Every roll was like slow motion," Inger remembers. "I heard the windows popping out. I hit my head and blacked out. The fire department had to cut the roof to get me out." Amazingly, the crash that should have killed Inger left her with hardly a scratch. "During the whole thing, I was praying I wouldn't die. It was amazing I didn't."

Two months later, Inger was in Atlanta competing in the Olympic relay. She watched as teammate Gail Devers streaked toward her, baton in hand, just ahead of the Jamaican and Bahamian teams. The two U.S. runners completed their exchange and Inger increased the team's lead, handing off to Gwen Torrence, who broke the tape with a time of 41.95 seconds. "All of us had terrible handoffs," Inger remembers. "If we'd had good handoffs, we would have set the world record."

As it was, they came within a half-second of the mark. Devers, Torrence, and Chryste Gaines—who ran the opening leg—joined Inger in celebration. Later, the four women mounted the winner's podium to accept their gold medals. As she listened to the *Star Spangled Banner*, Inger could not help thinking about her tortured road to victory. "What I've gone through is unbelievable," she says. "I always knew the ability was there, but I had to rebuild my confidence after the injuries."

Inger did not win a medal in the 200 meters, but her victory in the relay made both headlines and history. Never before had a father and daughter won Olympic medals. And never has a father had so much confidence in—or such a positive effect on—his daughter's track career. "Barring injury," Lennox says, "I think she can be the best woman sprinter in the world."

"It's been such a big plus to have my dad as my coach," says Inger, who has continued to turn in great times in the 100 and 200, winning six events in 1998. "The Olympic year was the foundation for everything."

Going forward, Inger's goal is to become the top-ranked woman in both the 100 and 200. "I want to be number one in the world, in both sprints," she says. If the law of averages counts for anything, that piece of good luck might just come her way.

No longer "Lennox Miller's daughter," Inger has an Olympic gold medal of her own.

ON HER MIND

"When I reach a goal, it pushes me to keep getting better and shoot for new goals."

If it were
easy
veryone would be ther

Angela Williams

Believe it or not, becoming a world-class sprinter can be a waiting game. When a young speedster believes she is a step away from greatness—when every dream she has ever had seems within her grasp—that is the time she must exert the most patience, and be willing to let her skills develop slowly.

Certainly, that has been the case for Angela Williams, America's most promising newcomer in the world of track and field. Born in 1980, she has accomplished much already, and has drawn comparisons to all-time greats Wilma Rudolph and Florence Griffith Joyner. Yet what impresses the experts most is not the national titles she has won, nor the records she has smashed—it is Angela's understanding of the timetable every great sprinter must follow.

"I know I have a long way to go," she says. "There's a lot more improvement I can make." That means something coming from someone who has been competing since the age of six, and setting records since the age of nine.

Angela developed her interest in running after her father volunteered to oversee a local recreation program in Chino, California. Johnny Williams hoped to keep kids off the mean streets of their Los Angeles neighborhood. He never dreamed that his young daughter would be interested. "I didn't want my baby girl running," he recalls. "I tried to tell

A hamstring injury kept Angels out of the 1996 Olympics. Her sights are now set on 2000 and beyond.

At 16, Angels already had the body of a world-class sprinter.

her to sit down. But some other adults involved said, 'Hey, just let the girl run—can't you see she's *beating* everybody else?'"

By the time Angela entered Chino High School, she had established nearly a dozen records for her age group. And college coaches were already expressing interest in her, even though she had never entered a high-school meet.

Angela's father, who worked for Chino High as a strength coach, continued to oversee her development. In 1995, she established a new mark in the 100 for freshmen with a time of 11.24 seconds—shaving a full third of a second off the previous record. A sore hamstring limited Angela's participation in short-distance races, so she began concentrating on the 400 and 800 meters. Johnny Williams believed that this would stretch out her muscles and give her added endurance as her body grew.

Angela did compete occasionally in the 100 meters. When she did, she dominated. It was fun smoking the other runners, but she understood that there was no reason to rush things. This became abundantly clear at the 1996 Olympic qualifiers. Angela had earned an invitation to the trials by virtue of her second-place finish at the Junior World Championships two weeks earlier in Chile. She wanted to run in the Olympics, and went all out in her first heat...and blew out her hamstring. "I felt good out of the blocks," she remembers, "but sixty or seventy meters out, it pulled on me and I fell to the ground, not able to feel my leg. Standing on the starting line and looking down that track just summed up my life and goals to that point. Then to tear a hamstring just ripped up all that. All of my dreams fell apart, so I had to really focus on rebuilding everything."

The next five months were spent rehabilitating her leg, and getting used to taking things easy. By the time her junior season began, Angela was confident, focused, and mature. Her goal in 1997 was to ease back into the 100, but secretly she wanted to break the national prep record of 11.13 seconds, which had held up for more than 20 years.

Getting Personal

Angela owes her athletic prowess to good genetics. Her mother, Pam, was a champion high-school sprinter in Mississippi. Her father, Johnny, was a star football player...Angela set a total of 13 national age-group records between the ages of 9 and 15... While in eighth grade, she coached an elementary school track team...While at Chino High, Angela sometimes visited area junior high schools and gave motivational speeches...In four years of high school, she never received a grade lower than an A...In 1996, Angela ran an indoor 500 meters race, and recorded one of the top 15 times in history...At a 1997 meet, she ran the 100 in 10.98. The mark is not recognized because it was wind-aided...Angela stands just 5-1$\frac{1}{2}$ and weighs a mere 115 pounds...The last athlete to be named Track & Field News High School Athlete of the Year twice in a row was superstar Marion Jones...During her off-seasons, she stayed in top form competing for the Southern California Cheetahs, an Athletics Congress team out of Walnut, California...Angela is a big believer in building toward a goal. "Achieving one aim gives me more confidence and courage to look

Career *Highlights*

Year	Achievement
1995	Set National High School Record, 100 Meters
1995	State Champion, 400 Meters
1996	Junior National World Champion, 100 Meters
1997	State Champion, 100 Meters & 200 Meters
1997	Pan Am Games Junior Champion, 100 Meters & 4 x 400 Relay
1997	Track & Field News High School Athlete of the Year
1998	State Champion, 100 Meters, 200 Meters & Long Jump
1998	Equals High School Record, 50 Meters
1998	National Prep Champion, 100 Meters
1998	Track & Field News High School Athlete of the Year

She came as close as you possibly could, turning in times of 11.14 and 11.15. Despite winning everything in sight that spring, Angela kicked herself for not setting a new record. "That drove me crazy," she laughs. "I asked myself, 'Could I have done some small things to get the record?'" Eventually, Angela came to realize that it was not worth getting stressed out. She would get the record when she was meant to get it.

The 1998 season brought to Angela all of the good things for which she had worked and waited. She won almost every race she entered, and tied the prep record for the 50 meters with a time of 6.32 seconds. In August, she went to Texas to compete in the U.S. Junior Nationals. She knew it would be her last chance to break the high-school mark for the 100 meters, but as she settled into the blocks and awaited the starter's pistol, she did something different: She *didn't* think about the record. Angela exploded off the starting line and kept picking up speed, winning the race easily. When she looked at the clock, it read 11.11. She had done it!

"People had never seen me get emotional and cry after a race," she says. "But after I finally got the record, I just couldn't hold it in. It came when I least expected it; in the last meet of my high-school career, when I had given up on getting the record."

Angela closed the book on her prep career and began to think about bigger and better things. After sorting through scholarship offers from every major track program in the country, she chose to stay close to home, and in the fall of 1998 started classes at the University of Southern California. The academics at USC are as exciting to her as the athletics. Angela was a straight-A student at Chino, and has her sights set on a medical career when her running days are done.

No one who knows Angela doubts that, one day, they will be calling her "Doctor" Williams. And the smart money says that, before she hangs a medical degree on her wall, there will be some Olympic hardware in her trophy case. Angela has the ambition, the talent, the heart, and the head. She also knows something her competition may not: Good things usually come to those who wait.

What lies ahead for Angela Williams? If she has her way, Olympic gold and a medical degree.

What's Next

T o the untrained eye, women's track and field appears to be going through a period of decline. "Where's the next Flo-Jo, the next Jackie Joyner-Kersee?" people ask. "Who are this generation's big names and where are they coming from?" The answer to these questions is that the next group of women's track and field superstars are just now beginning to emerge. And as fans will soon see, women's track is hardly in decline. In fact, this is a very exciting time for the sport.

A "warrior class" of athletes is being forged by the intense competition that exists today in women's track and field. These women know that a flawless performance from the mind and body sometimes is not enough, and they view "perfection" as something that can actually be improved upon. From this group, a select few will find a way to rise even higher. Just watch—they will begin to distinguish themselves in the year leading up to the 2000 Olympics, tinkering to find just the right blend of physical, mental, and technical improvement to sprint a quarter-second faster or leap a half-inch higher. Then, in Sydney, they will shift into high gear in front of hundreds of millions of viewers. From there, they will assume the awesome responsibility of defending their medals and maintaining their edge, as wave after wave of newly minted challengers attempt to knock them off their perch.

The woman who has already reached this high level, of course, is Marion Jones. Unfortunately, she has been cast by many in the media as the lone standard-bearer for her sport. That not only is unfair to other top track and field athletes, it could lead fans to develop unrealistic expectations for Marion. She certainly has the talent to dominate her events for many years, but there are some remarkable young women who will soon be pushing her. How Marion deals with this kind of pressure may ultimately determine how much time she (or her pursuers) shave off the records for the 100 meters and 200 meters.

If Marion Jones does manage to stay in the spotlight, she is likely to find it increasingly crowded over the next few years. Women's track is on the verge of a very special period in its history. There are a slew of world marks that are ready to fall—many of which have stood for more than a decade—and as every sports fan knows, nothing puts an athlete in the spotlight like breaking a record.

Thus we shall soon become acquainted with an entirely new generation of record-holders—not just in the 100 and 200, but in the 400- and 800-meter sprints, the 100-meter hurdles, the high jump, the long jump, the marathon, and the heptathlon. Fans need not worry where the "next Flo-Jo" will come from. There should be plenty of stars in the firmament as women's track enters the 21st century.

The real question is, whose will burn the brightest?

INDEX

PAGE NUMBERS IN ITALICS REFER TO ILLUSTRATIONS.